The Informal Encyclopedia of Regency Culture

Ellen Harveaux

Published by Ellen Harveaux, 2024.

While every precaution has been taken in the preparation of this book, the publisher assumes no responsibility for errors or omissions, or for damages resulting from the use of the information contained herein.

THE INFORMAL ENCYCLOPEDIA OF REGENCY CULTURE

First edition. October 16, 2024.

ISBN: 979-8227100511

Written by Ellen Harveaux.

Table of Contents

The Informal Encyclopedia of Regency Culture 1

Conveyances 51

Dances 52

Drinks 53

Foods 54

Inn names which appeared in modern fiction novels 57

Medicines and Maladies...58

Places of Interest 59

Regency Furniture Design Styles 62

Regency Romance Topics 63

Schools for Men and Boys 64

Social Concerns 65

Some Possible Plotlines 66

Streets of London that have appeared in modern fiction.................67

Towns which appeared in modern fiction novels 69

Tropes..70

Dedicated to my sister Beth.

You have been the source of many fond memories, the spice in our joint adventures and you have always been my closest friend. Best of all, you were and are the answer to my childhood prayers.

Contents

A-Z ENTRY PAGES

"ABIGAIL" TO "MRS. YORK"
BEHIND THE SCENES AND DEDICATION

REGENCY CULTURE

CONVEYANCES
DANCES
DRINKS
FOOD
INNS APPEARING IN MODERN FICTION
MEDICINES AND MALADIES
PLACES OF INTEREST
REGENCY FURNITURE DESIGN STYLES
REGENCY ROMANCE TOPICS
SCHOOLS FOR MEN AND BOYS
SOCIAL CONCERNS
SOME POSSIBLE PLOTLINES
STREETS OF LONDON
TOWNS
TROPES

A

Encyclopedia of Regency Culture and Common Expressions

Abigail-a lady's personal maid. Usually not a woman's name then at that era.

"A bit of muslin"-mistress.

Actor-Kean-famous male actor.

"Addlepated"-flustered.

Adventuresses-a fortune-hunting woman

A Fleet wedding-a fake wedding with a fake minister at a "marriage shop" near the Fleet River.

"Age of discretion"-old enough to know right and wrong, and liable for one's own conduct.

Aigrette-of creamy lace and russet feathers-a headdress for elite women.

Air- **"Turn the <u>air</u> blue with language"**-cursing.

"A kip"-for vagrants, a place to loiter in the neighborhood.

Almacks Assembly Rooms-ballroom on King St. Allowed a limited number of attendees. Patronesses were Lady Castlereagh, Lady Jersey, Lady Sefton, and Countess Lieven. They gave out vouchers to attend, with a strict dress code of evening dresses for women along with long gloves and stockings. Breeches, waistcoats, evening coats and gloves for gentlemen. In 1814, the Duke of Wellington was refused entry because he wore trousers. If granted a voucher, a young lady could be introduced to suitable partners. The waltz was not allowed in the ballroom. Entry was not based on wealth but on position in society. No liquor was served.

Alt- "been in the alt"-excited, happy (in the upper altitudes).

An Admiral's chair-a traditional leather executive office chair with a slightly sloped fully buttoned back. Arms were made of wood. Had six legs on rollers. Leather was dark, almost a burnished red. Tufted with nail and head trim.

"An Antidote"-someone who is viewed as a problem.

Andirons-a metal rack inside a fireplace to hold burning logs.

"An ice"-shaved ice with sweet toppings.

Annuity- "a Nootie"-lower class speech.

"Antecedents"-relatives.

"Anticipate the wedding"-have sex before the wedding.

Antipodes-Australia and New Zealand.

"Ape Leader"-a person others follow.

Aphrodisiac-a substance to increase sexual libido, sexual desire, or sexual attraction: oysters, dark chocolate, cloves, sage, alcohol.

"A pink of a ton"-a darling of the Ton.

"A plague on it"-a curse on someone.

Apothecary-an early druggist or pharmacist.

Appurtenance of wealth-trappings of wealth.

Arcane rules-complicated rules known only by a few.

Aristocratic hauteur-snobbery.

Artifice-devices to trick or deceive-make up, wigs, etc.

Assignation-an appointment to meet someone in secret, typically a lover.

Astley's-a theater which has acrobats, magicians, and trained ponies.

"A tyro on the ribbons"-a tyrant on the reins, an excellent driver.

Aubusson carpet-a flat-woven French carpet made for nobility and wealthy.

Australia-a place to ship convicts and criminals-called being transported to Botany Bay. A place to send rioters also.

Authors in Regency Era-Byron, Austen, Bronte, Mrs. Radcliffe.

Avuncular-a man acting like a loving uncle or grandfather.

B

"**Bad books**"- "I am in her bad books again"-they are angry with you.

"**Badly dipped**"-almost bankrupt.

"**Bag of moonshine**"-a lie.

Bagatelle-a game with small balls.

"**Bamming**"- "You're bamming us"-lying to us.

"**Banbury tale**"- "Fobbing me off with a Banbury tale"-telling a lie.

Bank notes-paper money.

Bantling-a young child.

Banyans-male lounging robes.

"**Barmy**"- "He was completely barmy"-completely crazy.

Baron-ranking higher than a lord or knight and lower than Viscount or count.

Baronet-lowest hereditary title. Usually called "Sir."

Barouche-four wheeled carriage with driver in high front seat, two double seats facing and folding top over back seat.

Barrister-a lawyer who only dealt with trials. Those who did not deal with trials were solicitors.

"**Barrow boy**"-a boy selling produce out of a wheelbarrow.

"**Bartholmew Fair**"-banned from causing public disturbances; a metaphor for chaos.

Bath chair-a rolling chaise for one with folding hood. A forerunner of a wheel chair.

Batman-a military aide.

Battle of Trafalgar-one of the most famous sea battles during Napoleonic wars. It was British Navy against Spain and France's Navies. Britian won. Admiral Nelson was commander.

"**Bawds**"-women brothel owners.

Beadle-the officer of the church who were to summon people to Parish councils.

Bearer bonds-note of debt security issued by a corporation or government.

Beau Brummell-a friend of George, Prince of Wales (Regent from 1811-then George IV) The leader of men's fashion.

Beau Monde-fashionable society.

"Beaux"-a boyfriend.

"Becoming inconvenient"-getting rid of mistress.

Bed curtains-curtains around a tester bed to close off sleeper from cold.

Bedlam-an institution for mentally ill.

"Bedlamite"-someone from a looney bin, Bedlam.

"Bed sport"-sex.

Beldame-a witch, malicious and ugly old woman.

Bell pulls-a woven pull cord which rings a service bell when pulled.

"Bête noire"-one or a thing who is particularly disliked. "Great Uncle Edward was my father's bte noire." Almost like a mimesis.

"Beyond the pale"-outside the bounds of acceptable behavior.

"Beyond reproach"-can do no social wrong.

Billet-nonmilitary housing for soldiers, usually in private homes.

Billet-doux-love letters.

Bilious color-the color of vomit-greenish yellow.

"Bird"-a woman.

"Bit of Restorative"-a dash of Brandy in a cup of tea.

"Bland"- "Bland as potato pudding."-unnoticeable.

Blas-jaded.

"Blighter"-a little boy.

"Bloke"-a man-lower class speech.

"Bloody hell"-cursing.

"Blue stocking"-bookish feminist.

"Blue devils"-becoming depressed.

Blunderbuss-first rifle. Most like a present-day shotgun.

"Blunt"-money.

"Blush"- "putting everyone to the blush"-embarrassing others.

"Bold piece"-someone very forward.

"Bolt-hole"-a place to hide.

"Boney"-old boney-Napoleon.

Bon Mots-a good word.

Bonnets-women <u>always</u> wore bonnets in public and mob caps at home.

Boot jack-a heavy metal tool that was shaped like the letter U that would pull a man's boot off his foot.

Boots- "half boots" for women made out of kid leather that reached above the ankle and below the knee.

Border Lords-Viking Raiders.

"Born on the wrong side of the blanket"-a bastard.

"Bossy boots"-a bossy girl.

Botany Bay-where criminals were transported in Australia.

"Bother"- "O Bother"-slang expression of frustration.

Bothy- "Decrepit bothy"- shanty.

Boudoir-a woman's bedroom or sitting room.

Boulanger-country dance.

"Bouncer"-a lie.

"Bounder"- "he's a complete bounder."-dishonorable man.

Bow Street Runner-fledgling private police force- "Runners" were paid for services by private citizens. They could arrest.

Boxing-usually practiced at Gentleman Jackson's. Also called pugilism.

Breeches-men's pants that end just under the knees.

Breeching-leather on inside of a coach.

Brown Study- "lost in a brown study"-lost in thought.

"Brush"- "hare's foot brush"-a rabbits foot brush to apply rouge.

Bumper-a bumper of burgundy-a glass filled to the brim.

"Bun fest"-what boarding school girls ate with other girls late at night.

Burke's Lineage-book detailing ancestry of peerage, baronetage and knighthood, first published in 1833. Genealogies.

"Bursting his stays"-men's corset was too tight.

Busk of a corset-a large stay inserted in front of the corset to keep it stiff.

"By-blow"-a child born out of wedlock. Also called, "born on the wrong side of the blanket."

"By Jove, By Jupiter, Zeus"-expressions of dismay or surprise.

"Bye the bye"-by the way.

"By word"- "hate to be a by word"-an adage, a motto, a catchphrase.

C

Cachet-prestige; admired.

Cad- "your behaving like a cad"-a man who behaves dishonorably.

"Cakes"- "making utter cakes of themselves"-make a fool of themselves.

Calling cards-small white cards with one's name engraved on it. It was left when visiting or to hand to new acquaintances.

Calumny-slander.

Cambric-dress material.

Cant-slang for lower class speech.

Caps-mob caps-worn over women's hair while indoors.

Card case-a metal case to hold calling cards.

Card games-Macao, faro, hazard, whist, brag, piquet, loo, and quadrille.

Card sharp-a cheat.

Carlton House-The Regent's London house.

Carriage four-in-hand-carriage with 4 horses.

Carriage ceiling trap-the door in the roof of the carriage to communicate with the driver.

Carte Blanche-an offer to a mistress by a man to become his mistress.

Carter-one who used his cart to transport boxes and luggage.

Cashiered out-dismissed from armed forces in disgrace.

Caster-sugar caster-container for sugar on table usually silver and part of a set.

"Cast him a speaking glance" -looking quickly and showing your annoyance.

"Cast up his accounts" -threw up.

"Cat"- "that would put the cat among the pigeons"-cause havoc.

"Catpurses"-pick-pocket or thief.

"Cat's paw"-under the cat's paw-a person bowing to the dictates of another-a mouse.

"Cattle"-horses.

"Caught a child"-gotten pregnant-lower class speech.

"Cavil"- "to cavil at annoyance"-make petty or unnecessary objection.

Cesspools-area under the outhouse or privy.

"Chalk and Cheese"-as alike as-opposites.

Chamber pot-a bowl in the bedroom used as a toilet.

Chamber robe-a robe for the bedroom.

Champagne blackening-used on Hessian boots to make them shine.

Charity- "out of charity" with someone-angry with someone.

"Charnel"- "What a charnel house that battlefield was. (Waterloo)-indicative of death.

Cheerful cretonne cushions-printed cotton.

Chemise-a loose fitting slip.

Chemisette-a small cambric scarf to cover area above a low neckline.

Cheval glass mirror-tall mirror on a stand.

Chicken skin fan-used to decorate an ivory fan. Painted with ornate scenes.

Chilblains-sores from exposure to extreme cold.

Chinoiserie-Chinese motif.

Chintz-a material for upholstery.

"Chimney pots"-earthenware or metal deflector over the top of chimneys to reduce smoke.

"Chit"- young chit-a young girl.

"Chit tendre"-tender notes.

"Cicisbeos"-a married woman's lover, much like a man's mistress.

Cit-not nobility, citizen, in the trades.

"City bronze"-or Town bronze-acquiring proper manners of London.

"Cleaned out"-has no money.

"Clich"- "Distressing to be a cliché"-overused.

"Clod pate"- "What a clod pate"-lacking in common sense.

Clubs-Men's clubs-White's, Brooke's, Watier's-exclusive to ton.

"Clutch"- "a clutch fisted employer"-stingy.

Cob-a groom's horse.

Cobblestones-mostly used in rich neighborhoods.

"Cock-a-hoop"-pleased with success.

"Cock up his toes"-died.

Coiffeur-a woman who styles hair for females.

Collar points-collar points that covered his ears-style for Dandies.

Comeuppance-taken down a peg or two.

Comestibles-anything edible; food.

"Commission"- "bought his commission"-paid to become an officer in the army.

"Complete crackbrain"-crazy.

Comtesse-a French Countess.

Cong- "he got his cong"-rejection.

"Continent"-the continent of Europe.

Constable-local police.

Constabulary-early police also added Scotland Yard and Bow Street Runners.

"Convenients"- "using the servants as convenients"-using them for sex.

Coppices-places where trees or shrubs are cut back.

"Coquette"-a game-a tease.

Coquettishly-being a flirt and a tease.

"Cor"-expressing surprise-lower class speech.

"Cord"- "he pulled the cord"- a way to signal the coach driver to stop.

Corinthians-gentlemen who were active in sports; athletic.

Cornets-ornaments on carriages to show nobility/peerage, Family crest.

Cortege-a funeral procession.

Corset-regular corset laces in the back. Cannot be put on without a maid. Or taken off without a maid's help.

Cosset-take tender care of, pamper or spoil.

Costermonger-one who sells vegi's and fruits.

Cottage orn-rustic building.

"Coterie"- "Coterie of Gentlemen"-people with shared interests.

Counterpane-a bedspread.

Countess-wife of an Earl.

"Country Dowd"- "to look a country Dowd"- older woman without style or social sense.

Coup de grace- the blow that kills.

Courier pigeons-homing pigeons.

Courtesan-prostitute with wealthy clients.

"Cove"-slang for a nobleman or gentleman-lower class speech.

"Cow's eyes"- "making cow's eyes at you"-wide-eyed expression, with unstated romantic attraction.

"Coxcomb"-a foppish dandy.

"Coz"-a short for cousin.

"Coze together"-to chat.

"Cozen"- "Don't cozen me"- try to trick or deceive.

Crack- "we're all the crack"- we wear all the latest fashions.

"Cracked"- "cracked in the nob"- crazy in the head.

Cravat-men's starched ties around the neck made of white linen.

Crenellations-the battlements of a castle.

Crony-a close friend.

"Crossing sweeper"-a lad or someone who swept horse droppings from the streets so people could walk unhindered. They were paid with tips from those crossing the street.

"Crossing the Rubicon"-a decision with irreversible consequences.

"Cropper"- "to come a cropper"-to fail; be struck by some misfortune.

Crupper-the part of the saddle where a second rider would sit behind the primary rider.

"Crypt"- "Got the look of the crypt about you"- Looks like you need to be buried; dead.

"Cub"-young cub-young aristocrats.

Cuckold-a man whose wife is unfaithful.

"Cuckoo in the nest"-a throwback to a previous relative's looks or personality.

"Cur"-a mongrel dog who's aggressive.

Curly-brimmed Beaver top hats for men-died black.

"Custom"- "you'll lose my custom"-you'll lose my business.

"Cut direct"-out-right snub.

"Cutting a dash"-looks attractive in smart clothes.

"Cyprian"-a mistress.

D

Dab hand- "She has a dandy hand at baking."-a person who is an expert at a particular activity.

"Daffy"- "to much daffy last night"-slang for Gin.

Dalliances-casual romantic relationships.

"Dally"- "dally with her"-a casual romantic liaison.

Dame school-a home school for young children taught by a local woman for a fee. Usually when young boys were to poor for rich school.

"Damn & blast"-favored oath.

Dancers-opera dancers-a whore; opera singer was an artist.

Dance set-three dances in a row.

Dandy-a man unduly devoted to style and clothes.

"Dark walk"-a secluded path at Vauxhall-garden for lovers.

"Dash"- "cutting a dash in London"-looking fashionable.

"Dawn appointment"-a duel.

Dclass-low in social class.

Dcottetage-low neckline.

"Deep in Dun Territory"-to much debt to pay back.

"Denizens of brothels"-customers.

"Derigueur"- "a low neckline is derigueur"-required by fashion etiquette or court rules.

"Dernier cri at court"-fashion to wear-to be presented at court.

Desk Acoutraments-1. A Quill. 2. A Penknife to trim nib (quill point) 3. Sand for blotting letters. 4. A heavy roller to blot page after document is finished. 5. A metal seal to impress into melted wax. 6. A small metal dish for melting sealing wax. 7. A trash bin for used sand.

Dtrop-feeling unwelcome.

"Deuce take it"-The devil take it, deuce is synonymous with the name Devil.

"Devil take it"-cursing- (anything with word devil in it).

"Devil's bones"-dice.

"Diamond of the First Water"-exceptionally beautiful.

"Dilettante"- "idle dilettante"-a person with amateurish interest in the arts.

Dimity-curtains hung on four poster bed-sheer cotton fabric with raised stripes or checks.

"Directions"- "did he leave his new directions"-his address.

Directoire style of dress for women-Paris styled dresses-sleeves are puffed; high waisted.

"Discretion"- "past the age of discretion"-competent to exercise good judgement.

Dishabille-scantily clothed.

Disoblige-offending someone.

"Dismals"- "in the dismals"-distressed.

"Dismissal"-"without character"-fired without references.

Dissimulation-pretense; hiding true thoughts or feelings.

"Dissipated"- "led a dissipated life"-overindulging in sensual pleasures.

Distingue-distinguished.

"Dog in a manager"-someone who selfishly withholds from another what he doesn't need.

"Dogs body"-a person who is given boring, menial tasks to do.

"Doing it a bit to brown"-trying to defeat someone.

"Done up"-without funds.

"Don't give a fig for"-don't care what people think.

"Dotage"- "in their dotage"-old and weak.

Dormeuse cap-a sleeping cap-(French) for women.

Dowagers-matrons, heir's mother.

Dower house-the new home of the widow of previous heir who died.

"Doves of Venus, soiled Doves"-prostitutes.

"Doxy"-lover or mistress.

Drafts-financial checks.

"Dragooned"- "I could have dragooned you into coming with me"-forced you.

Dragoons-mounted infantry with Red Coats.

Drawers-underwear.

Drays-low cart without sides.

"Dreaming Spires"-Oxford.

"Dropsical"- "he appeared dropsical"-has dropsy, swollen under the skin.

"Drubbing"-beaten up.

Drum- "following the drum"-wives who follow their soldier husbands into the fields of battle.

"Ducks"-Darling, Dear-lower class speech.

Dudgeon- "high dudgeon"-to flounce or storm off in a temper fit.

Duels-legal until 1819.

Duke-member of royalty or nobility.

Duke of Wellington's staff @Waterloo-1. Lord Fitzroy Somerset-W's military secretary. 2. Sir Charles Stuart-Brit Ambassador to the Hague.

"Dull as ditchwater"-extremely dull.

"Dull pudding"-block head.

"Dun Territory"- "notoriously close to Dun Territory"-broke.

"Dutch courage"-drunken courage.

E

Earl-British nobleman above a Viscount and below a Marquess.

"East End" of London-overcrowded, unsanitary, with squalid living conditions. Called "The Stews."

Eeau de nil silk gown-pale greenish gown.

Effete-affected and overly refined.

Epergne-ornamental centerpiece for fruit or flowers for dining table.

"En fete"-in a festive mood.

Engage antes-false sleeves on gowns to lengthen elbow length sleeves.

Ennui-boredom, indifference.

Entailed-an inheritance law that settles property over a number of generations so ownership stays in the same family.

Equerry-an officer in the household of a noble who had charge of the stables.

Escritoire-a small ladies writing desk with drawers and compartments.

Escutcheon-coat of arms on carriage, front door, etc. to denote nobility.

F

"Facer"- "plant him a facer"-hit him in the face.

Factotum-aide-de-camp.

"Fancy"- "the fancy"-a sporty young gentleman; lower class speech.

"Faradiddle-of a come-out-pretentious nonsense.

"Farrago"-a confused mixture of fact plus fiction; a partial lie.

"Fashion"-First stare of Fashion-at the forefront of fashion.

"Fashionable salons"-meetings of artistic society interested in poetry.

"Fast"-loose, improper behavior; scandalous.

"Featherbrained creature"-silly, nonsensical.

Femme de manage'-house maids.

"Fencing piste"-the marked off area to fence.

Fender-the frame that keeps fireplace wood in the fireplace.

Fens-the marshlands, bogs.

"Fey"-Something fey about her-other worldly.

Fichu-small triangular shawl worn around a woman's shoulders and neck.

"Fiddle"-in a fiddle-uncertain.

"Fillet"-a gold fillet in her hair-a twist of metal and cloth for the hair Roman style.

"Fine as fivepence"-as fine as possible.

"Fire"-if we're going to fire you off...-introduce you to the ton.

"Fishwife"-a coarse shouting woman.

"Flagrante Delicto"-caught in the act of sexual misconduct.

Flambeaux-flaming touch by front door at night.

"Flapping my gums"-talking too much.

"Flea"-you'll send me off with a flea in my ear-a sharp reproof.

The Fleet-subterranean River in London.

Flint and Tinder-used to start a fire.

"Flummery"-empty compliments, nonsense.

Flunky-a liveried footman.

"Fobbed off"-change the subject with a lie.

Fobs- a small ornament attached to watch chain.

"Folderal"-trivial or nonsensical fuss.

Foolscap-large size of paper about 13x8 inches.

"Footpads"-a criminals on foot-street criminals who usually hunted in pairs-a highway man on a horse.

"Fops"-a Dandy who only cared about fashionable clothes.

Fortnight-two weeks.

"Foxed"-drunk.

Franking postage on letters-the stamp price-duty that was already paid by nobles.

"Free trade"-smuggling.

French émigré's-French families in England whose sons fought Napoleon.

"Fribble"- "Her mother dismissed the man as a fribble-of little importance.

Frills- "You know how girls are always out looking for frills and gewgaws."

"Fringes"-bangs on women's hair.

"Fripperies and foibles of the ton life"-showy ornaments and eccentricities.

Frogging-military braid on women's clothes usually on a riding habit-Chinese knots that fastened the jacket.

Frowsty carriage-stale, stuffy, warm atmosphere.

"Full fettle"-I need you in full fettle-good health.

"A fulminating look"-a denouncing or menacing look.

"Fusspot"-fussy person.

G

"**Gadfly antics; japes**"-one who attacks people with criticism.

"**Gaining your majority**"-becoming an adult, age 18 or 21 depending on law.

Gainsaid-to deny or contradict a fact or statement.

"**Gallows bait!**"-a person who would make you so angry you'd want to murder them, sending you to the Gallows.

Gallows humor-ironic humor in hopeless situations.

Game- "Hunt the Hare"-spy game for children.

Gamester-a gambler.

"**Standing around like a gape seed**"-without any real goal.

Gauche girl-socially awkward.

"**Gave his horse the office to start**"-gave the kick to start riding.

Gazette-London newspaper.

"**Gel**"-a girl or young woman.

"**By Gemini**"-An exclamation using mythological characters. Zeus is a favorite.

Gentlemen's gentleman- a valet.

Gentry-the class of people blow nobility in position and birth.

Gibbet-execute by hanging.

"**Gilding the truth**"-lying.

Glaring pugnaciously-threatenly.

"**Gossip mongering**"-those who spread rumors.

"**Got plenty of bottom**"-courage.

Governess-an impoverished, educated woman from a good family. She was expected to teach and train young boys and girls in education and deportment. Older boys, had male well- educated, poor tutors, for the same subjects.

"Grande Dame"-an older woman of Ton with an influential position. A doyenne.

Greatcoat-long woolen overcoat designed for warmth and protection from elements for men.

Groat-a small coin/sum. "I do not care a groat." Don't care at all.

Groom-for ladies on a horse. A groom follows to assist and be a chaperone.

Groom's horn-blowing for the tall gate to open for oncoming carriages and mail coaches.

"Gull"-what kind of gull do you take me for? Duped or deceived person.

Gunters-a place for shaved ice topped with sweet syrups.

"Gutterscum"-the poor.

"Guttersnipes"-a scruffy and badly behaved child who spends most of their time on the streets.

Gypsy Bonnet-a bonnet, wide brimmed straw hat with ribbons tying under the chin.

H

Habeas Corpus-a writ that a person under arrest be brought before a judge or into court, especially to secure a person's release unless lawful grounds are shown for their detention.

"Hackney"-old carriages used like taxis, can be hailed or picked up at a hackney stand. Sometimes called a hack.

"Hades"-a curse.

Halcyon-happy and peaceful days in the past.

Half-mourning dresses-half way through the mourning period women could choose to stop wearing black and wear lavender or gray dresses.

"Half turned"- half turned the key-half-heartedly.

Halves- "She never does anything by halves."-she is very thorough.

"Ham fisted"-trying too hard; too obvious.

Handfasting marriage-a legal marriage over anvil in Gretna Green Scotland. No license needed.

"Happenstance"- "It was no happenstance."-no coincidence.

"Haring off"-Running off in an uncontrolled way, like a rabbit.

"Harridans"-scolding, even vicious old woman.

"Harpy"-mythical monster that was half woman and half bird; evil.

"Hash"- "He had made a terrible hash of this."-messed it up.

"Hatches"- "under the hatches."-without funds.

Haute Monde-fashionable society.

Haute Ton-fashionable, elite; elegant.

Hauteur-arrogant attitude; snobbish or smug.

"Havey-Cavey"-unsteady.

Hazel switch-used for whipping a child.

Headstrong-stubborn; impulsive.

"Heady brew"- "It's a heady brew."-exciting, rash and impetuous.

Heartshorn-smelling salts.

"Hell"-a gambling establishment.

"Hell's teeth"-a curse.

Hessians-glossy black boots for men. Military looking. Some had gold tassels to be more elegant.

"High"- "He was top of the trees."-he reached highest level of society.

"High-flyer"-high class prostitute.

"High impure"-high class prostitute.

"High in the instep"-overly proud or arrogant of one's social standing.

"High ropes"- "get on your high ropes"- get on your high horse.

"High sticklers"-have ultra-high standards of behavior.

"High Toby"- "Am I playing the high toby?"-taking the high road.

Hip bath-a portable bath tub, usually small and made out of copper or cheaper metals. Usually moved to bedroom and filled by the footmen or maids with pitchers of hot water. User cannot stretch out and their knees stay under their chin.

"Hob"- "the soup boiled on the hob-a metal hot plate on the stove.

Hoby's-high-end boot maker for men.

"Hoi polloi"-the common masses.

"Hoity-toity"-snobbish, upper-class person-lower class speech.

"Hole in the corner"-being secretive.

Holland covers-linen to cover unused furniture. Linen was made in Holland.

"Holy of holies"-Almacks Assembly Hall.

"Honest"- "Has he offered us honest coin about her?"-has he told the truth about her.

"Honey trap"-a woman who will trap a man into marriage.

Horseguards-British secret service.

"Horses"- "The horses jibbed."-horses balked and refused to go forward.

Horse's curb bit-a bit that injures a horse's mouth to keep them in line.

Horseshoe staircase-rises on two sides.

House party-a coed party for the ton generally held in a country home. It usually lasts almost a week with entertainment.

"How much"- "How much of the ready had you paid?"-what was the cost?

"Hoyden"-a wild young girl; a tomboy; a boisterous girl; uncontrolled girl.

"Hunting boxes"-hunting lodges for men only.

"Hum"- "It's all a hum."-a lie.

Hussar-army that wore a red military uniform.

Hussars-were light cavalry used for scouting and raiding.

Hyde Park-see Special places.

I

"I am not feeling quite myself at the moment"-feeling ill or out of sorts.

Imbroglio-an embarrassing situation.

Ingenue-unsophisticated young woman.

Inglenook-a chimney corner in a recess that adjoins the fireplace.

In loco parentis-when an adult acts in place of a parent.

Inns of Court-each of the four legal societies with exclusive right of admitting people to the bar.

Insouciant-casual lack of concern; indifference, bored.

Interregnum-a period when normal functions of government are suspended.

Invalid cup-a cup with a long spout on top like a straw for the sick.

Iron carriage wheels-an upgrade from wood. Used in Regency London by rich.

"I shall put inquiries in train immediately."-I will start inquiries at once.

"Issue"-offspring.

"I won't be a tick."-a minute.

J

"**Jade**"-a disreputable woman.

"**Jacknapes**"-an impertinent person.

Jacobin philosophy-Radical revolutionaries led to the Guitellora, who planned French revolution and the down fall of the king-leader Robespierre.

"**Jape**"-mockery or practical joke.

"**Jarvey**"-man who drives a hackney.

Jerkin-a sleeveless leather men's jacket; vest.

Jewel casket-a small ornate box to store small amounts of jewelry.

Jointure-an estate settled on a wife for the period she survives her husband.

Jore de vivre-love of life.

K

Kennels-a small ditch in the middle of the street for all the detritus of the street to drain away.

 "**Knave**"-She saw a great deal of the <u>knave</u> about him. - dishonesty.

 "**Knocker on the door**"-meant owners were in residence. If gone the knocker was removed.

 Old fashioned knot garden-herbs planted in the shape of a knot

L

Landeau-see conveyances.

Lappets of her cap-long sides that hung over ears.

Laudanum-liquid opium.

Lawn-fine material for sheets, men's shirts and women's underwear.

"Laying in"-having a baby.

Leading strings-used on toddlers to keep them from running away from nurse or parent; leash.

"Left on the shelf"-an old maid.

"Leg shackled"-marriage.

Lending library-early library where people could check out books for a small membership fee.

Levee-an embankment near a river's edge.

"Libertine"-a man who behaves without moral or principles especially in sexual matters.

"Life sentence"-marriage.

"Light-o-love"-wanton woman.

"Lightskirts"-prostitutes.

Link boys-boys who carry flaming torches or lanterns while walking rich partygoers from coach to front door.

Lisbon-in 1811 where Wellington gathered troops to fight Napoleon's army in the Peninsula.

"Lists"- "Ready to enter the lists"- ready to engage in conflict.

"Little Season"-September to November before Christmas.

"Little tart"-immoral woman.

Livery-uniforms worn by staff of the rich. Each house was usually color-coordinated choosing their own unique color choice.

Longcase clock-Grandfather clock.

Loo mask-half masks for masquerades.

Lout-ruffian.

Lorgnette-a woman's pair of glasses held in front of her eyes by long handle on one side.

"Love match"-those who marry for love not money or social position.

"Love sick"-"love sick moon calf."

"Lunnon"-London-lower class speech.

Lynch-gate-covered entrance to Church yard.

M

Machinations-a plot or scheme, usually evil.

"Mad as a March hare"-crazy.

Maître-master (swordsman).

Mail coach-a stagecoach used to deliver mail and poorer customers. Had strange hours and stops to hand off mail bags.

Majordomo-chief steward of a large household.

Marlborough Palace House-east of St. James Palace.

Malingerer-to fake an illness to avoid work or duty.

Magistrate-a lay judge who rules over minor offences in a small area or location of authority.

Man of business/affairs-a man who was hired to handle someone's affairs and family's business, much like a personal secretary or administrative assistant. It was never a woman's job.

Mantra maker-modiste, seamstress.

Mantons-where gentlemen learn to shoot guns.

"March"- "Stolen a March on her"-gain an advantage over someone by acting before they do.

"Mare's nest"-a muddle, a mess, an illusory discovery.

Marquess-nobleman ranking above an Earl and below a Duke.

"Marriage mart"-the season where young women made their "come out" to find a husband.

Marriage Settlement-documents drawn up by a couple's fathers, spelling out financial interests of both parties before ceremony.

Mary Wollstonecraft-a prominent feminist who wrote "A Vindication for the Rights of Women."

Mayfair-an area bordering Hyde Park, an upscale area.

"Mayhap"-maybe.

"Mawkish"-sentimental in a sickly way.

"Mealy-mouthed"-to speak frankly.

"Megrims"- "we all have our megrims"- depression.

Mlange - "a drifting mlange of perfume"-a mixture, a medley.

Mercer-one who sells cloth.

"Mettle"- "I felt on my mettle"-needing to prove ones worth.

Mews-a large area behind mansions where stables were kept; also carriages.

"Midden"- "smelled as bad as a midden."-dung hill.

"Milksop"-one who lacks courage; indecisive, timid.

"Mill"-a fight.

Minerva Press novels-Mrs. Radcliff's Gothic romances.

"Minx"-a bold, flirtatious girl.

"Miss"- "a milk and water miss."-someone prim and proper.

"Missish"-squeamish; prudish.

Missive wafer-a small gummed label to seal a letter.

Mohacks-a gang of violent, well-born criminals that terrorized London in early 1800's.

Mon amie-my friend (French).

"Moonling"-a simpleton; a lunatic.

"More the thing"- "I hope you are feeling more the thing."-hope you are feeling better.

"Morning calls"-calls were made between 2pm and 4pm.

Mountebank-a person who deceives people, in order to trick them out of money.

Mounting block-a tall square block of wood in the stable yard to help a woman mount her side-saddle.

Muniment room-document room in rich homes.

Musicale-an evening of musical performances.

N

"**Nabobs**"-gentlemen who got rich in India.

Nadir- "fly from alt to nadir in but moments."-the lowest form of sufferings.

"**Naf**"- "She's not a naf."-naive.

Nankeen- "a boy in nankeen trousers."-yellowish cotton.

"**Necessary**"-the toilet inside the house usually behind a screen in bedroom with a chamber pot.

"**Neck or nothing**"-daredevil riders.

"**Needle witted**"-clever.

Neuralgia-intense intermittent pain along nerve in head or face.

Nib-tip of a quill pen that needed to be kept sharp with a small knife.

"**Niggled**"- "It niggled her"-bothersome in a tiresome way for thoughts.

"**Night humors**"- "bad to let the night humors in"-belief that night air brought disease.

"**Nightman**"-a man who empties outhouses called cesspools-done at night. Also called night soil collector.

"**Night rail**"-nightgown.

"**Nine day's wonder**"-something that attracts great interest for a short while then is quickly forgotten.

"**Nines**"- "She was dressed to the nines."-to perfection.

"**Ninny-hammered wives**"-a fool or simpleton.

"**Nip farthing**"-a stingy person, a miser.

"**Nodcock**"-dense; fool or idiot.

Nonpareil-no match or equal.

"**Nonce**"-prison slang for sex offenders.

Non-sequitur-a conclusion or statement that does not logically follow from the previous argument or statement.

Nostrums-a medicine not considered effective prepared by an unqualified person.

Nurse-baby's nanny.

O

"Odd's teeth"-astonishment.

"On dit"-up to date rumors and gossip.

"On Original"-woman who stood out from rest in a Season. Unlike anyone else.

"The Ordinary room"-the downstairs room at an inn where the common people gathered. See public room.

Ostlers-those who handle the horses at an inn where carriages change horses to continue on their travels.

Outré- "going out of style."

Overset-upset.

P

Paid companion-a woman who was hired to attend to and go in public with a rich older woman who usually was a widow living alone.

Pantalets-long underpants with a frill at the bottom of each leg, worn by women and girls under dresses.

Pantaloons-men's pants tightly fitted down to the ankle.

"Panting"- "another panting hound"-suitor becoming obnoxious.

Paramour-lover.

Parlor boarders-day students in boarding school.

Partirre-a place for planting ornamental flowers.

Parure-a matching set of three or more jewelry pieces.

Pas de deux-an intricate relationship involving two parties.

Pattern cards and Pattern cards of propriety-cards with needlework that must fit on a printed pattern. Also a metaphor for society's rules or social patterns.

"Pay the shot"-pay the bill.

Peccadillo-a small sin.

Peerage-aristocrats.

Penury-extreme poverty.

Pelisse-a woman's narrow coat with armholes or sleeves reaching to the wrist. The coat covers length of long dresses.

Pembroke table-small 4-legged table having two drop leaves and a drawer.

Persona non grata-a person not wanted.

Peste-a pest, a troublesome person or thing.

Phantasms-ghosts.

"Pillion"-a secondary riding pad, seat, or cushion behind the saddle on a horse for a 2nd rider.

Pince-nez-eye glasses that are supported on nose by them pinching the nose to hold them in place.

"Pinchbeck"- "you're offering pinchbeck for gold"-an alloy used in costume jewelry.

"Pipe dreams"-opium drugged dream.

"Piquant look"-a charming look.

"Pistol"- "a pistol at the ready"-a gun primed to shoot.

Pittance-small amount.

Plebian blood-commoner; lower class.

Plinth-a heavy base supporting a statue or vase.

"Plump"- "we are not plump in the pocket"-we are almost broke.

"Pockets to Let"-a poor single gentleman who is asked to attend dinner parties to even out the genders seated at the table for a free meal.

Point-non-plus-a situation with no options.

"Polite circles and Polite world"-high society.

"Popinjay"-peacock, featherbrained man.

Porringer-a small bowl with a handle for soup or stew.

Porte-Porte cochere-a large covered entrance porch to park under.

"Portentous"-overly portentous-behave more seriously to impress others.

"Portion"-a dowry.

Portmanteau-a large trunk or suitcase opening in two equal parts.

Posset-cream, eggs, sugar and wine, a liquid for sick; upset stomach.

Post boys-boys who rode leading horses for a post chaise which had no drivers. Was a faster way to travel.

Poste restante-general delivery post office.

Postilions-boys who rode horses for a post chaise.

Posting house-an inn where coaches changed tired horses for fresh ones.

"Postprandial cigars and port"-what men did alone after dinner before joining the ladies.

Postprandial doze-a nap after lunch or supper.

Pot boy-boy in kitchen who scrubs pots.

Pox- "riddled with the pox"-Syphilis.

"Priggish"-high morals, judgmental and arrogant.

"Prinny"-Prince of Wales-was the Regent for his father hence the name "Regency" period.

Prior-the head of a priory, an abbot or father superior.

Priory-monastery.

Privateer-an armed ship owned and officered by private individuals holding a government commission able to engage in war for their country.

Privy-outhouse.

"Proletarian politics"-working class people's politics.

Promenade-stroll or a place to stroll.

Propriety-having acceptable morals and behaviors.

"Public room"-at the Inn. A place where the commoners would, eat, drink and wait for the mail coach. The rich ate in private dining rooms.

"Purse pinched"-broke.

Q

"Queer the pitch"-the act of ruining or interfering or spoiling something.

Quill-feather pen for writing.

Quizzing Glass-a single lens on a handle when held up before the eye to enable closer scrutiny of the object or person in view. Used by rich men to intimidate. Usually hung on a silk cord around the neck.

R

Rabbit- "stop looking like a rabbit heading for the pot"-terrified.

"Rack and ruin"- "go to rack and ruin"-fall into disrepair.

Racy inclinations-titillating behavior.

"Raddled complexion"-red pocked skin of a drunk.

"Rake"-a man who lacks moral or sexual restraint.

"Rakehell"-man who is morally unrestrained.

"Rake of the first stare"-a high-brow womanizer.

Rapiers, Epe-swords.

"Rattle"- "not a dullard"-You're a rattle, maybe"- confused and upset.

"Ready"- "How much of the ready did you put into it?"- the money.

References-servants needed references to find a job. If they did a poor job they could be fired or without references, which meant they could not get another job.

Regent-a person appointed to administer a country because monarch or a minor is incapacitated.

"Regimentals"-military uniforms.

"Rejoinder"- "he restrained himself from the swift rejoinder that came to his lips"- swift comment.

"Relict"- "a relict of her husband"- a widow.

Rendezvous-a romantic meeting.

Repast-a meal.

"Requiring satisfaction"-a duel.

Retainer-a servant who has been with the family for a long time.

Reticule-a small bag-like purse that hangs off a woman's wrist.

"Ribbons"-reins.

"Rich as Croesus"-Croesus had legendary wealth.

Ridottos-public entertainment.

"Ring a peal over his head"-to scold.

Riot Act-if read aloud to crowd, soldiers could shoot or bayonet the crowd if they didn't disperse.

Riposte-a quick, clever reply to an insult or criticism. In sword play a return thrust to a parry.

Risqu-slightly indecent.

"River Tick"-in deep debt.

Rogues-scoundrels.

"Rotten Row"-an area in Hyde Park where high society went at 5pm to ride on horses or carriages to see and be seen.

"Rotter"- "he was a rotter"-evil.

"Rous"-aging rakes.

"Rough justice"-street justice.

"Rouleau of guineas"-a cylindrical pack of coins.

Round gown-a dress with an over-gown; a dress without a train.

Routs-a crowded party.

"Rubbed along well enough"-to work or play with little or no difficulty.

"Rubbish"-unbelief, not true.

"Rum"- "it was all very rum"-strange.

"Rushed"- "I rushed my fences"-acted hastily.

Rustication-leave city for country temporarily for welfare, health reasons or in debt.

S

"**Sacked**"-fired.

"**Sacrifice**"- "a daunting air of sacrifice"-martyr.

"**Salad days**"- "he was wild in his salad days"-young and inexperienced days.

Salle-room for sword fighting practice.

"**Salon**"- "a salon"-a afternoon meeting in a woman's house usually about poetry, or art.

Saloon-a large room intended for large gatherings.

"**Salt**"- "any man worth his salt would..."-someone who will go the distance, is worth the cost.

"**Sanctimonious prig**"-a self-righteous person.

Sans culottes-a lower class Parisian or an extreme revolutionary.

Sarcenet-a material-silk with a bit of stiffness.

Sardonic glint-mocking or cynical look.

"**Saucy minx**"-a pert, sexy, strong, outgoing woman or girl.

Saville Row-a Street for handmade tailoring for men.

"**Scandal broth**"-rumors; gossip.

"**Scandal sheet**"-cheap newspaper about Ton gossip and rumors.

"**Scapegrace**"-a rascal-mischievous.

Scion-a descendent of a notable family.

Scrubwoman-woman who used bucket and mop to clean.

Scull-oars used by a single rower.

Scullery maid-a servant who washes dishes.

Sealing wax-hot wax to seal letters with a monogrammed stamp or coat of arms.

Season-coincided with Parliament in session-November to May-also called Marriage Mart. "Small Season"-September to November.

Secretaire-a small writing desk.

Sedan chair-an enclosed chair for one person, carried on two poles by two men.

Sennight-a week.

Serpentine-a river along the side of Hyde Park.

Servant's stairway-usually narrow stairs that were near the kitchen so servants could go upstairs to clean etc. without using the family's public staircase.

Serviette-a napkin.

"Set down"-turn one's back on or snub someone silently- "a cut direct" is a verbal put down.

Setting up your nursery"-for men getting married and starting to have children.

Settles-wooden benches in an inn or ale house.

Sevres China-French true porcelain made near Versailles.

"Shade"- "he's going to put me in the shade"- outshine me.

Shako-a military style hat for women or men-usually tall.

"Shamming"-teasing.

"Shank's"- "to ride Shank's pony instead"-reduced to walking.

"Sharp"- "she's as sharp as a thorn and blunt as a cudgel"-smart and cutting.

"Sharp set"- "a guest who is sharp set"-hungry.

"She's a prime article"-she's a good catch; a good looker.

Shift-a woman's slip worn under a dress.

"Shooting a quelling look"-a look to stop one in their tracks.

Sidesaddle-a saddle for women which allows women to sit aside rather than sit astride.

Silver salver-the plate on the hall table of a mansion's foyer to collect letters or calling cards.

Sinecure-a very easy job.

"Sixes and Sevens"-chaos.

Sizzled-drunk.

"Skivvy"-a servant.

Slop bucket-a bucket in the bedroom where used washwater was dumped.

"Sloven"- "I look a thorough sloven"-messy, dirty.

Small clothes-underwear.

"Smoky"- "I'm sure she thinks there is something deeply smoky about..."-some dark secret.

"Snuff"- "I'm up to snuff"-meeting the required standards.

Social solecism-behavior making a social mistake.

Society Maven-an expert on society's rules and regulations. Usually a woman.

Soirees-an evening party.

Solicitors-a lawyer who deals with the public, not trials.

"Som 'at"- "a bit of Som 'at to eat-something to eat-lower class speech.

"Sortie"-an attack.

Sovereign-a gold coin.

"Speaking glance"- "she gave him a speaking glance"-a glare.

Special license-a marriage license gotten quickly through a Bishop for a rushed marriage.

Spencers-a woman's short jacket to wear with high waisted gowns. Jacket stopped at the high waist.

"Spiking their guns"-to prevent someone from carrying out their plans.

"Spinning me a tarradiddle"-telling a lie.

Spinster-unmarried women.

"Spoiled doves"-loose women.

Sponging house-debtor's jail.

Sport- "a bit of sport"-sex.

Squabs-the pillow part of a carriage seat.

Standish-inkwell holder.

"Station"- "those not knowing what was due their station"-nobles who did their own chores.

"Stays"-bone structured garments worn under gowns; corsets. Usually said about men, "busting their stays"-too fat.

Steward-one who oversees an estate's business.

"Stews"-the stews where the poor and criminal element lived in London. The East End.

Stillroom-where homemade medicines were kept-the rich bought their medicines.

"Stretching"- "they were stretching their ears"-they were trying to eavesdrop.

"Strict rules"- "old tabbies"-older Ton women who insisted on strict rules for others.

"Stripling"-a young man or boy.

"Struth"-It's the truth.

Stygian gloom-unpleasantly dark.

Superfine-high end material for men's coats.

"Summat"-something (slang) lower class speech.

Subaltern-an officer in British army below the rank of captain.

"Suffered fools gladly"-won't put up with foolishness.

Succubus-a female demon-believed to have sex with sleeping men.

Subscription-subscription library-an early form of lending library for members.

"Swells"-the rich aristocratic men. A term used by lower class for rich.

Swiving-have sex with-lower class-slang.

Swordstick-a sword hidden in a cane.

Syllabub-warm milk, wine, sugar and spices to ward off colds.

T

"Taking her up"-paving the way for someone to be accepted into Society.

Tambour frame-a frame to work on embroidery. Frame stands on floor.

"Tan"-the Tan-a sand path that ran alongside the paved coach path in Hyde Park for horse riders.

Tantalus-a small liquor cabinet that locks.

Tartar-one with a violent temper.

Tea Caddy-a wheeled tea cart.

Teasel-a plant in the honeysuckle family.

"Ten a penny"-cheap.

"Tendre"- "developing a tendre for someone"-have romantic feelings for someone.

Termagant-a harsh overbearing woman.

"Terror"- "the Terror"-the French Revolution.

Tertian ague-Blackwater fever-malaria.

Tester bed-canopy bed.

"Thames Wherry"-a rowboat or barge on the river Thames.

"Throw"- "throw your hat over a windmill"-to fall in love.

Tiger-a groom for a gentleman, who rides behind curricle on a little stand on the back.

Tilbary-a light, open, two wheeled carriages with or without a top.

"Tinker's"- "don't give a tinker's damn"-don't care what people think.

"Tipple"- "a pint of ale is more my tipple"-more my drink.

"Toadeater"-to stroke another's pride, ego. (We call them brown nosers.)

"Toast"- "a toast"-a Toast of the Town.

"Toffs"-a aristocrat-low class speech.

Toll roads-tall gates which barred the road until road users paid toll.

"Ton"-the fashionable society.

"Tongue"- "I gave them the length of my tongue, I did"-a tongue lashing.

"Toplofty"-haughty and arrogant.

"Topsy Turvey"-head over heels.

"Toque"-a woman's hat with a narrow closely turned up brim.

"Torn"- "I knew I'd torn it for sure"-I knew I'd lost my chance.

Tosspots-drunks.

Tot-a tot of Brandy-a dash of Brandy.

"Town"-London-always capitalized.

Trade- "going into trade"-members of the Ton starting their own business. It was a scandal that blackened their family name. Gentry or lower *could go into trade*.

Traditional times-when nobles mingled with commoners: Harvest time, Christmas, Twelfth Night, May Day on estates in the country.

Trap-a small two-seater pony cart.

Traveling trunk-leather and brass bound large trunk.

"Treacly"- "listening to conversations so treacly it makes one's teeth ache-false sweetness.

"Trice"- "in a trice"-in a moment.

"Trod"- "trod the boards"-was an actor or actress.

Trollop-female prostitute-low class.

Trompe l'oiel-French style painting mostly on ceilings or furniture.

Trug-a long open basket to lay cut flowers in, with an oval or oblong shape.

Tryst-romantic rendezvous.

"Tumble"- "having a tumble"-an unmarried couple having sex.

"Turnout"- quite a turnout he's driving-a great conveyance.

"Twaddle"-foolish speech or writing; nonsense.

U

"**Under the table**"-drunk.

    "**Up in the boughs**"-angry, irritated.

    "**Upper Ten Thousand**"-high society members.

V

Vails-gratuities paid to serving staff by household guests at a noble's house party.

Valise-suitcase.

Vellum-calf-skin parchment paper.

Venetian breakfasts-held any time before 1pm.

Verger-an official in a church who acts as caretaker and attendant.

Vicar-a minister in charge of a church who serves under the authority of another minister.

Virago-a domineering, violent, or bad-tempered woman.

Viscount-ranking above a Baron, below an Earl.

Vouchers-IOU's. See vowels.

"Vowel's"-IOU's given when a gentleman loses while gambling.

Vulpine-curving of his lip-crafty, cunning.

W

Wager-"I wager this."-I bet it is.

Waistcoat-a vest.

Ward-an orphaned child one protects and houses, until they reach their majority.

Washstand-a large pottery bowl on a wooden stand which holds hot water (from maid) to wash up. Some had mirrors attached. There were also wooden racks to hold towels and wash cloths.

Wastrel-good-for-nothing person.

Watch- the watch-neighborhood patrols looking for foot pads to arrest them.

Water Butt-water barrels.

"Watering pot"- "reduce me to a watering pot"-incessant crying.

Waterloo-town where Napolean met his defeat in Belgium (near Brussels) in 1815.

Waterman-one who transports people on the river Thames.

Water steps-steps down to the river Thames to enter a boat going down or across the river.

Waybill-for public coach-a ticket to ride.

"Wear the willow"- "Do you wear the willow for him?"-long to reunite with a lost love or deceased love.

Welsh dresser-China hutch.

"Wench"-tavern maids.

"Wenching"-consorting with prostitutes in ale houses.

Weston's-the company name of makers of high-end clothes for men.

"Where the devil? - what the devil!"-cursing.

"Whey faced"-pale from fear.

"White slavery"-where women are stolen for prostitution.

"Widgeon"- "Don't be a widgeon!"-a fool.

"Winsome"- "a pretty winsome piece"-nice looking woman.

"Woman of easy virtue"-mistress.

Workhouse-a place where poor were kept to work off their debts.

Wrapper-a long bathrobe for women.

Y

"Yellow boy"-gold coin.

    "Yer"- "you" low class speech.

    "Mrs. York"-writer of horrid novels.

Conveyances

Barouche-a large, open four wheeled carriages drawn by 2 horses, holds 4 passengers. Driver sits on a high box seat. Four passengers in back had an overhead folding hood.

Brougham-a horse drawn carriage with a roof, four wheels and driver's seat in the front.

Curricle-a open, two wheeled gentleman's carriage where riders sat high and was pulled by 2 horses abreast. If there was one horse, it was called a chaise.

Gigs-a light 2 wheeled, one horse vehicle for two passengers.

Hackneys-Regular family carriages were recycled to be used as taxis.

Landau-a 4 wheeled carriage with 2 folding hoods that meet over the middle of passenger compartment.

Phaeton-a sporty light, open four-wheeled horse drawn carriage. It had no side protection and a seat so high one must use a ladder to reach the seat.

Post chaise-four-wheeled, closed carriage for 2 or 3 passengers. There was no driver. One or two "drivers" rode on the horses"

Trap-a one horse, one or two passenger cart with 2 wheels.

Dances

Allemande-a waltz-like dance with intricate passing figures.

Boulanger-a simple circle dance for a group of couples.

Contradance-a couple's dance in 2 long facing lines.

Cotillion-8 dancers of 4 couples in a square-a forerunner of a Square Dance.

Minuet-a slow graceful dance in ¾ time, characterized by forward balancing, toe-pointing and bowing.

Morris Dancing-English folk dance usually by men who do choreographed moves. Sometimes call Mummers. They sometimes have bells below their knees. Usually performed outside on town streets around Christmas.

Quadrille-a dance with 4 couples with each couple forming a single side of a square.

Scotch reels-a dance that has 2 steps: stepping in place then weaving in and out of lines made by other dancers.

Strathspeys-a slow Scottish dance for 4 or 5 couples with some sliding steps and a bounce step.

Waltz-a dance of two partners close together. They went forward, backwards counting by threes and twirling.

Drinks

Ale
"Blue Rum"-cheap ale house drink.
Brandy
Brandy with spiced milk.
Burgandy
Canary wine
Champagne
Claret
Coffee
Cognac
Cowslip wine
Elderflower wine
Grog-watered rum.
Madeira
Negus-wine mixed with sugar water.
Port-Porter
Rack punch-served at Vauex Hall Gardens.
Ratafia
Renish
Sherry
Spiced wine-wine with cloves and nutmeg.
Tea

Foods

Breads

Wheaton bread

    Cakes
    Tansy cake
    Desserts
    Blancmange-sweet dessert.
    Charlotte Russe
    Damson tarts
    Flummery
    Puddings-currant and rice.
    Syllabub
    Eggs and Cheese
    Cheese flan
    Custard tarts
    Kedgeree-kippers, rice and egg dish.
    Plover's eggs
    Rhenish cream
    Stilton-blue cheese.

    Fish and Seafood
    Carp
    Eels
    Kippers
    Lobster patties
    Lobster mousse
    Oysters
    Oyster patties
    Scalloped oysters

Stewed fish
Trout
Fruit
Candied fruit
Crystalized fruit
Spiced pears
Light meal
Cold collation-cold meats, sauces, fruit, bread and nuts.
Meats
Bacon
Black Pudding-blood sausage.
Boiled beef
Ham
Kidneys
Lamb collops
Mutton chops
Sauteed calves' livers
Savory tarts
Sirloin
Sweet meats
Veal and ham pie
Poultry
Duck
Pigeons
Pigeon pie
Quail
Roasted chickens
Roasted Partridges

Salads
Sparrow grass salad
Soups and stews

Barley broth
Mutton stew
Rabbit stew
Turtle soup
Vegetables
Asparagus
Buttered parsnips
Creamed leeks
Green fritters-made of peas or Swiss chard.
Porringer-a compote of mushrooms.

Inn names which appeared in modern fiction novels

Angel Inn
Black Lion
Blue Duck
Dragon
Fox and Hounds
George
Green Man
Hare and Hounds
King's Arms Inn
Lamb and Flag
Red Fox
Red Lion
Rose and Crown
Shakespeare's Head Tavern
The Bell
The Coach and Horses
The George Inn
The Gull
White Hart Inn

Medicines and Maladies

A tincture-a slight trace of a drug in alcohol.

A tisane-a drink of water-based herbs, spices, flowers and leaves.

Heartshorn-smelling salts.

Pastilles-lozenges for sore throats.

Quinsey-sore throat from infected tonsils.

Vinaigrette-3 parts oil to one-part balsamic vinegar.

Sal volatile-smelling salts.

Sack Posset-lemon or citrus juice, cream and sugar. Eggs are often added. Sometimes bread crumbs are added to thicken the beverage. Spiced wine was added to kill germs. Used to ward off colds.

Places of Interest

Bank of England

Berkeley Square

Billingsgate Fish Market

Bond Street

Bridewell

Carlton House-a mansion in Westminster best known as the town residence of George IV.

Covent Gardens, The Piazza

Custom House

Dover-seaport.

Drury Lane Theatre- London's West End theatre.

Fencing Studio, boxing clubs

Greenwich Observatory-seaport.

Gretna Green-destination for eloping couples just across the border in Scotland. No clergy or license needed.

Grosvenor Square

Houses of Parliament

Hyde Park-Rotten Row-The Tan-in Hyde Park.

Lions in the Exchange

London Bridge

Long Acre

Marshalsea-debtor's prison.

Martin-in-the-Fields

Newgate Gaol

Pall Mall

Piccadilly

Portman Square

Ranelagh

Richmond

Richmond Park-grassy area along the Thames.

St. George's Church-Hanover Square.

St. James Palace

St. James Park

St. Paul's Cathedral-Anglican Episcopal Church.

Stanhope Gate

Tattersalls-horse sales happened on Mondays.

The Fleet-debtor's prison.

The Stand

The Tower of London

Theatre Royal-iron spikes around stage-orange sellers.

Vauxhall Gardens

Westminster Abbey

White's-a gentleman's club in St. James, London, in Mayfair District.

Whitehall-center of British Government.

Regency Furniture Design Styles

Chinese-included ornate wallpaper and lots of black lacquer furniture.

"Ebonized wood"-to darken a light wood to give it the appearance of ebony, a sleek jet-black exterior.

Egyptian-pyramids seen in designs.

Etruscan-furniture from a culture absorbed by Rome which was heavily influenced by Greek.

French-Louis XVI-gilt furniture.

Greek-Baroque, Federal Directoire, Georgian era and Neo Classical.

Indian subcontinent-furniture brought back by rich Nabobs, including statues of elephants, monkeys, Indian gods and goddesses.

Mahogany-main woods: ebony, rosewood, and zebra wood.

Roman-heavily influenced by expeditions and archaeological discoveries in England.

Symmetry-clean lines, rectangles came into fashion in all furniture.

Check out this website:

Showrooms2220.com

History and characteristics of Regency Style Furniture.

Regency Romance Topics

·Independent heroine must bend to strict social rules she despises.

·A Season packed with balls, and vicious gossip, that newcomers must navigate.

·Happily-ever-after with a reformed rake who is a Duke, Viscount or Earl.

·Carriage rides, morning calls, routs, plays, assemblies, picnics, balls, and other activities.

·Seducing the Duke.

·Reforming the Rake.

·Fake relationships-false engagements.

·Fake identities, amnesia, personal vendettas.

·An unmarriageable woman, for one of the many reasons but who finds love anyway.

Check out Top Tropes of Romance Literature: Regency Edition Thriftbooks.com

Schools for Men and Boys

Cambridge-a legendary university that has King's college and King's chapel.

Eton-largest boarding school for boys in England. Boys went to Eton from age 13 and graduating at age 18.

Harrow-a boarding school for boys age 13 to 18 before they attend University.

Oxford-a university famous for its libraries. It is the 2nd oldest in the world.

Social Concerns

1. Rights of women.
2. The Poor.
3. Slavery.
4. Medicine.
5. Inheritance laws.
6. Heavy Taxation because of War with Napoleon.
7. Orphans.
8. Chimney sweeps.
9. Child labor.
10. Waterloo Vets who were homeless and destitute.
11. Napoleon trying to conquer Europe.
12. Transportation.
13. Smog and it's health ramifications.
14. Education of the poor and women.
15. Disease that had no cures. Malaria and Syphilis.
16. Quacks and Charlatan's with seances and fake cures for ailments.
17. Death in childbirth.
18. Unsanitary surgeries.

Some Possible Plotlines

·A betrothed woman falls in love with someone else before her wedding.

·To marry a rich man for status or poor man for love.

·An innocent woman is compromised and must marry someone immediately that she does not like or want.

·Two sisters fall in love with the same man.

·An independent young beauty refuses to even meet the man her parents have chosen for her to marry, but she accidently encounters him and falls in love.

·Marry a woman to gain a child back-from 1st wife's in-laws.

·Woman must marry in a fortnight or lose property and house where she is harboring the poor and orphans.

Streets of London that have appeared in modern fiction

(Names of streets found in N.Y. Times Bestselling authors)

Adam's Row
Albemarle
Aldersgate
Berkeley St.
Brook St.
Bruton St.
Cavendish Square St.
Chancery Lane St.
Charles St.
Cheap St.
Curzon St.
Dean St.
Devonshire St.
Duke St.
Fleet
Goodge St.
Gray's Inn Rd.
Half Moon St.
Henrietta Place
Holles St.
King
Lauriston St.
Millicent Row St.
Moor St.
Mortimer St.
Mortimer St.
Mount

New Market
Peel St.
Pickering Place
Portman Square
South Audley St.
Stafford
Stratton St.
Threadneedle St.
Upper Brook
Upper Brook St.
Wigmore St.
Wigmore St.
Wimpole St.

Towns which appeared in modern fiction novels

Bankside
Basingstoke
Cheapside
Cheswick
Christchurch
Dover
Hammersmith
Kensington
Knightsbridge
Lymington
Winchester
York

Tropes

Time Frame
British Regency 1811-1820

1. Marriage of convenience.

2. Scandal and forbidden love.

3. Separated lovers reunite.

4. Romances with Dukes.

5. Beauty and Beast.

6. Makeover Story.

7. Compromising situation.

8. The Governess is attractive.

9. Bad boys.

10. The boss and under-appreciated female worker.

11. Enemies to lovers.

12. Amenesia.

13. Best friend's sister or sudden lovers who have known each other as children.

14. Woman disguised as a male meets a man she wants.

15. Fairy Tale retelling-Beauty and the Beast, Cinderella, Pygmalion, Robin Hood, Rapunzel, Sleeping Beauty and Ugly Duckling.

16. Arranged marriage-people from warring clans fall in love and are separated.

17. Forbidden Fruit.

18. Duty and Honor rather than love.

19. Love on the Road (or any adventure.)

20. Love Triangles.

21. Secret Identity.

22. Rags to Riches-unknown orphan inherits and displaces another heir.

23. Royalty and Commoner.

24. Second Chance meeting again.

25. Secret Baby.

26. Unrequited Love.

27. Missing heiress or heir.

28. Man must marry an heiress to save the family but falls in love with a poor woman.

About the Author

Ellen has been writing since she was 8 years old. She is a career teacher and a teacher at heart.

Ellen's hobbies are water color painting and loving on her cats.

www.ingramcontent.com/pod-product-compliance
Lightning Source LLC
Chambersburg PA
CBHW071232130726
47998CB00002B/921